Sally

OPENED
DOORS

By **Sandy Eisenberg Sasso** • Illustrated by **Margeaux Lucas**

APPLES & HONEY PRESS

*"Her ways are ways of pleasantness and
all her paths are peace." (Proverbs 3:17)*

*For those who paved the way and for all who walk on it.
— S.E.S.*

*For Mom, also a Sally, who opened many doors for me.
— M.L.*

Apples & Honey Press
An Imprint of Behrman House Publishers
Millburn, New Jersey 07041
www.applesandhoneypress.com

ISBN 978-1-68115-592-0

Library of Congress Cataloging-in-Publication Data
Names: Sasso, Sandy Eisenberg, author. | Lucas, Margeaux, illustrator.
Title: Sally opened doors / by Sandy Eisenberg Sasso ; illustrated by
  Margeaux Lucas.
Description: Millburn, New Jersey : Apples & Honey Press, [2022] | Summary:
  "Sally Priesand, the first American woman to be ordained a rabbi, opened
  doors for Jewish women's full participation in Jewish life, in this
  third book by Sandy Sasso about courageous women from Jewish history"--
  Provided by publisher.
Identifiers: LCCN 2021052843 | ISBN 9781681155920 (hardcover)
Subjects: LCSH: Priesand, Sally--Juvenile literature. | Women
  rabbis--United States--Juvenile literature.
Classification: LCC BM755.P725 S27 2022 | DDC 296.8/341092
  [B]--dc23/eng/20211206
LC record available at https://lccn.loc.gov/2021052843

Design by Alexandra N. Segal
Edited by Dena Neusner
Printed in the United States of America

9 8 7 6 5 4 3 2 1

Sally walked up to the podium to begin the Shabbat service.

"Who is that?" a visitor asked, a little too loudly.

"That's the rabbi," his friend whispered.

"A woman rabbi? Outrageous! You start opening
the door to change, and this is what happens."

The whole congregation heard. Everyone stared at Rabbi Sally.

It was the 1970s, and doors were opening for women all across America.

They could be doctors,
lawyers, even pilots.

But two thousand years of tradition
said that only men could be rabbis.

Sally took a deep breath, opened her prayer book,
and began leading the service in her clear, strong voice.

After services, she greeted everyone.
One of her students asked, "Didn't you want
to yell at that man? Weren't you angry?"

Rabbi Sally shook her head. "If all the space in your head is filled with anger, you have no place for anything else. A rabbi has so much to do. There is no time to waste."

Back in her office, Sally remembered when she had
first decided that she wanted to become a rabbi.

She was sitting in the sanctuary of her childhood synagogue.
She loved the prayers, the Torah dressed in velvet and silver,
the congregation singing together.

She watched as the rabbi led services and spoke out for what was just and kind. And she imagined herself on the *bimah* doing just that. She leaned over to her friend and whispered, "One day that will be me in front of the congregation, carrying the Torah, giving the sermon. I am going to be a rabbi!"

Her friend's jaw dropped. "Sally, are you serious? Look around! Women serve coffee, tea, and cake after services. They teach children. They never lead prayers; they never take out the Torah. Haven't you noticed that only men are rabbis?"

Sally smiled. "For now."

When Sally returned home, she knew what she had to do: not just learn Torah, but teach it; not just listen to a sermon, but give one; not just sit in the congregation, but lead it.

Her heart pounded as she sat at her desk and slipped
a piece of paper into her typewriter. Her fingers
pushed the keys carefully. *Clickety clack, clickety clack.*
There could be no mistakes.

Dear Sirs,

I am writing to ask about coming to your rabbnical
school.

I am sixteen years old. I love everything about
being Jewish - holidays, ritual, prayers, traditions.
I am the only Jew in my school, and I am always asked
to explain what it means to be Jewish.

I want to study to become a rabbi. Please let me
know when I can visit and learn more.

Sincerely,

Sally Priesand

Every day Sally would run to the mailbox to check for
an answer to her letter. Days passed, then weeks.
Her dog, Shadow, pranced alongside her.

Sally was ready to give up hope when, one month later,
a letter did come. She tore open the envelope.

Her hands were shaking.

Shadow's ears perked up as
she began to read aloud.

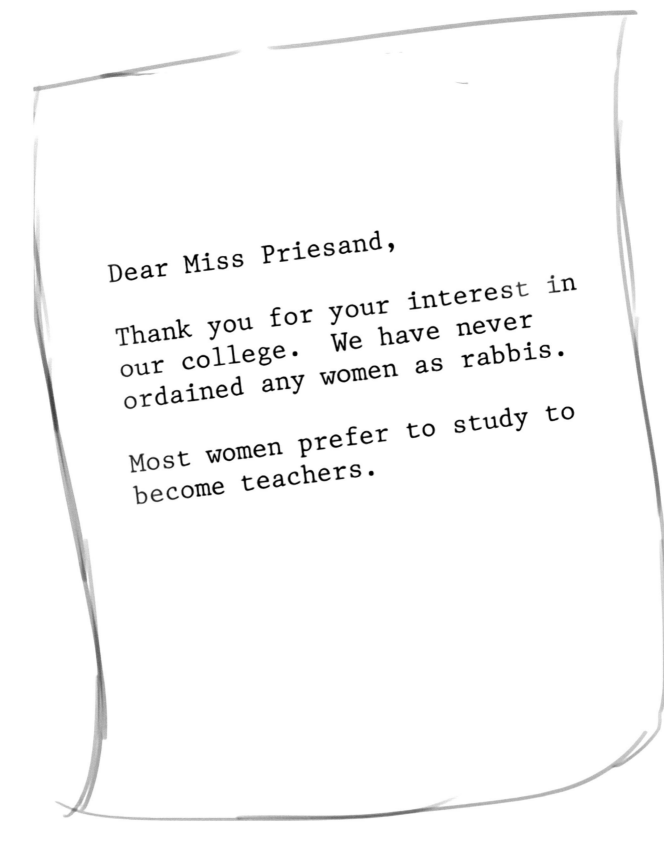

Dear Miss Priesand,

Thank you for your interest in
our college. We have never
ordained any women as rabbis.

Most women prefer to study to
become teachers.

Sally frowned, and Shadow nuzzled his nose against her cheek. She assured him, "No woman has been ordained as a rabbi *yet*. But I am going to change that."

Years later, she did—Sally didn't give up on her dream. She applied to the rabbinical seminary, and she was accepted. When she walked through the doors, there were no other women there. On her first day, the professor looked around the class and said, "Welcome, gentlemen!"

He was not the only one who hesitated to welcome Sally.
People whispered:

"She is only here to find a husband."

"No congregation will hire her."

"She will never finish."

But Sally did. She finished her studies. Finally, she became a rabbi. Not all congregations welcomed her, but one did.

A knock on Rabbi Sally's office door
startled her out of her memories.

A young woman entered and began, "Rabbi Sally, the first time I sat in your congregation and heard the tapping of heels on the *bimah*, I looked up. There you were—a woman rabbi! That moment changed everything. I now know what I want to do. I want to be a rabbi . . . like you."

She paused before continuing, "But I'm worried. I heard what that man said at services: 'A woman rabbi? Outrageous!'"

Sally smiled. "Don't worry about what others say. If I had, I wouldn't be sitting here. People told me I would never be a rabbi."

"Didn't you worry that they might be right?" the young woman asked.

Sally continued, "I did, at first. People were always looking over my shoulder, waiting for me to make a mistake. But I had a worry rule: 'Sit down for ten minutes every day and worry as much as you want. And then, get up and get on with it.'"

The young woman got up
and got on with it. She too
became a rabbi. And she
wasn't the only one.

Young women heard Sally
speak; they saw her picture in
newspapers; they read articles
about her in magazines.

Sally Priesand.

Mothers shared the articles with their daughters.
Some of those daughters grew up to be rabbis.

When those women graduated, they thanked Sally.

"If it weren't for you, I wouldn't be a rabbi."

"You were the first woman rabbi I ever met."

"You opened the door."

"And you walked through it!" Sally responded.

Sally continued to speak up and speak out.
One day, a little boy had a question for her,
one she had never heard before.

"Rabbi Sally, can boys be rabbis too?"
Sally smiled and nodded.

Dear Readers,

I wonder if you have a dream for your future. Is there something that you really want to do, even though people tell you that it cannot be done?

Sally dreamed of being a rabbi at a time when there were no women rabbis. Despite criticism and challenges, she persisted in fulfilling her dream. She became a role model for many women.

I wonder who are your role models. How might you become a role model for someone else?

Rabbi Sally loved everything about her religious tradition. What about your tradition do you love?

Sandy Sasso

Rabbi Sally and her dog

Rabbi Sally J. Priesand, America's first female rabbi, finished her rabbinical studies at Hebrew Union College–Jewish Institute of Religion in June 1972. At that time, there were no women teaching at seminaries and few Jewish women leaders. One of the professors would not sign her diploma. Congregations were reluctant to bring a woman to their pulpits. She was the last person in her graduating class to be offered a job.

Rabbi Priesand became the assistant rabbi at a large synagogue in New York City, where she served for seven years, but when the congregation was ready to hire its senior rabbi, she was not even considered. For two years she was not able to find a synagogue willing to accept a woman as its only rabbi. Then in 1981 she became the rabbi of Monmouth Reform Temple in New Jersey, where she served for twenty-five years, until her retirement, upon which she became rabbi emerita.

Rabbi Sally Priesand became a leader in the Reform movement; she introduced inclusive God-language into worship; and she worked on behalf of the poor, the hungry, and the homeless.

Thirty-seven years before Sally, another woman, Regina Jonas, had become a rabbi in Berlin, Germany, but her story was forgotten for a long time. With Sally, a new era began for women who wanted to become rabbis. Two years after her ordination, the Reconstructionist Rabbinical College ordained Rabbi Sandy Eisenberg Sasso (1974). The Conservative movement ordained Rabbi Amy Eilberg in 1985, and Open Orthodoxy ordained Rabba Sara Hurwitz in 2000.

There are more than a thousand women rabbis in the world today.